Washington, D.C.

by Patricia K. Kummer
Capstone Press
Geography Department

Content Consultant:
Jane Freundel Levey
Editor
The Historical Society of Washington, D.C.

CAPSTONE
HIGH/LOW BOOKS
an imprint of Capstone Press

C A P S T O N E   P R E S S

818 North Willow Street • Mankato, Minnesota 56001
http://www.capstone-press.com

Library of Congress Cataloging-in-Publication Data
Kummer, Patricia K.
    Washington, D.C. / by Patricia K. Kummer (Capstone Press Geography
Department).
        p. cm. -- (One nation)
    Includes bibliographical references and index.
    Summary: Provides an overview of the nation's capital, including its
history, geography, people, and living conditions.
    ISBN 1-56065-684-0
    1. Washington (D.C.)--Juvenile literature. [1. Washington (D.C.)]
    I. Capstone Press. Geography Dept. II. Title. III. Series.
F194.3.K86 1998
975.3--DC21
                            97-40351
                               CIP
                                 AC

Editorial Credits: Editor, Martha E. Hillman; cover design and illustrations, Timothy
    Halldin; photo research, Michelle L. Norstad
Photo Credits:
Archive Photos, 25; Mark Wilson/Reuters, 39
Betty Crowell, 14
Dembinsky Photo Assoc. Inc./Gary Meszaros, 5 (bottom)
Digital Stock, 6, 9, 28, 34, 40, 46
Thomas R. Fletcher, 10
GeoIMAGERY/Hermine Dreyfus, 17, 19
International Stock/John Cardasis, cover; Johnny Stockshooter, 30
One Mile Up, 4 (top)
Unicorn Stock Photos/Dick Keen, 5 (top); Joe Sohm, 22; Karen Holsinger, 33
Visuals Unlimited, 20, 26; William J. Weber, 4 (bottom)

Table of Contents

Fast Facts about Washington, D.C.

District Flag

Location: In the eastern United States, between Maryland and Virginia along the Potomac River

Size:
   68 square miles (176.8 square kilometers)

Population:
   543,213 (1996 U.S. Census Bureau estimate)

Wood thrush

American beauty rose

Founding date: President George Washington chose it as the site for the nation's capital in 1791.

Nicknames: The Nation's Capital, The Capital City

District bird: Wood thrush

District flower: American beauty rose

District tree: Scarlet oak

Scarlet oak

Chapter 1

The National Mall

More than 20 million people visit Washington, D.C., each year. Visitors come from all over the world. Most of them spend time on the National Mall. A mall is a long, grassy area. Tourists visit buildings and monuments along the mall.

The Two Ends of the Mall

The U.S. Capitol stands at the east end of the mall. A capitol is a building where lawmakers meet. Visitors can watch these lawmakers at work.

U.S. representatives and senators make the nation's laws in the Capitol. U.S. citizens

The U.S. Capitol stands at the east end of the National Mall.

choose people to speak for them in Congress. These people are representatives and senators. Congress is the governmental body of the United States that makes laws.

The Lincoln Memorial stands at the west end of the mall. Visitors look at the marble statue of Abraham Lincoln. The monument honors the 16th president of the United States.

The Middle of the Mall

The Washington Monument is located in the middle of the mall. The monument stands between the Lincoln Memorial and the Capitol. It honors George Washington. He was the first president of the United States.

The Washington Monument is the tallest building in Washington, D.C. Buildings in the district cannot be taller than the Washington Monument. Visitors ride an elevator to the monument's top. They look out over the city.

The Nation's Capital

Washington, D.C., is the nation's capital. A capital is a city that is an official center of

The Lincoln Memorial honors Abraham Lincoln.

government. Washington is the headquarters for the U.S. government. Washington is the only city in the nation that is not part of a state. Washington is in a district. D.C. stands for District of Columbia.

Washington is the only city in the District of Columbia. At first, Washington covered only a part of the District of Columbia. Today, the city spreads over the entire district. Washington, D.C., covers 68 square miles (176.8 square kilometers).

Chapter 2

The Land

Washington, D.C., is in the eastern United States. Two states border Washington. Maryland borders Washington on three sides. Virginia lies southwest of Washington. The Potomac River separates Virginia from Washington.

Atlantic Coastal Plain

The Atlantic Coastal Plain covers two-thirds of eastern Washington, D.C. Marshes once spread across parts of this land. A marsh is an area of low, wet land.

The Anacostia River flows through the coastal plain. It empties into the Potomac River.

Rock Creek flows into the Potomac River.

The lowest point in Washington is on the Potomac River. It is only one foot (0.3 meters) above sea level. Sea level is the average level of the ocean's surface.

In some places, low hills rise above the coastal plain. Capitol Hill is one of them. It stands 88 feet (27 meters) above sea level.

The Piedmont

Northwestern Washington, D.C., lies on the Piedmont. Piedmont means at the foot of a mountain. This land is higher than the coastal plain.

Rock Creek marks the beginning of the Piedmont. The creek winds through northwestern Washington. It flows into the Potomac River.

The highest point in Washington is on the Piedmont. It is 410 feet (125 meters) above sea level.

Parks, Woods, and Wildlife

Washington, D.C., has about 150 parks. Rock Creek Park is in the northwestern part of

Washington. Dogwood, beech, and cedar trees grow there. Wood thrushes and scarlet tanagers nest in the trees. Deer also live in the park.

Potomac Park lies along the Potomac River. The Tidal Basin cuts into the park. A tidal basin is a low area near a river that takes in flood water. Japanese cherry trees line the Tidal Basin.

Theodore Roosevelt Island is in the middle of the Potomac River. Willow, ash, maple, and oak trees grow on the island. Foxes, squirrels, and raccoons live there. Theodore Roosevelt was the 26th president of the United States.

Climate

Summers are hot in Washington, D.C. The temperature there is sometimes more than 90 degrees Fahrenheit (32 degrees Celsius).

Washington has mild winters. Winter temperatures usually range from 30 to 60 degrees Fahrenheit (-1.1 to 16 degrees Celsius). Washington usually receives little snow. About 16 inches (41 centimeters) of snow falls there each winter.

Chapter 3

The People

In 1994, Washington, D.C., was the nation's 20th largest city. Between 1990 and 1996, its population dropped by about 10 percent. The city lost more than 63,000 people. Today, about 550,000 people live in Washington.

Washington has some problems. It has a high crime rate. It also has problems in its schools. The city offers few jobs for people who do not work for the government. Some Washingtonians have to work outside the city. A Washingtonian is someone who lives in Washington, D.C. Some people work in Washington but live in nearby towns.

Today, about 550,000 people live in Washington.

Temporary Washingtonians

Some people live in Washington, D.C., for only a few years. About 41,000 of those people are citizens of other countries. They work at their countries' embassies. An embassy is a building where representatives from another country work.

Some government workers live in Washington for a short time. They include the president, the president's family, and some of the president's staff. U.S. senators, U.S. representatives, and some of their staffs are also in this group. They come to Washington when Congress meets. They go home for the rest of the year. They continue coming to Washington while they are in office.

African Americans

African Americans have lived in the area that is now Washington, D.C., since the 1600s. Early African Americans were slaves. Most worked on tobacco plantations. A plantation is a large farm. Later, many slaves and free African Americans helped to build the new nation's capital.

By the 1800s, freed slaves also lived in Washington. About 11,000 free African Americans lived there by 1860.

Today, about 66 percent of Washingtonians are African American.

During the Civil War (1861-1865), more African Americans arrived. Many were slaves who escaped from other states. President Lincoln freed all slaves in the District of Columbia in 1862.

Today, about 66 percent of Washingtonians are African American. Washington has one of the highest percentages of African Americans among major U.S. cities.

European Ethnic Groups

About 30 percent of Washingtonians are white. Washington has a lower percentage of whites than most U.S. cities. The Foggy Bottom and Georgetown neighborhoods have the largest white populations.

Most white Washingtonians have European backgrounds. Many of their families came from England, Ireland, and Germany.

Hispanic Americans

Hispanic Americans are one of the fastest-growing groups in Washington, D.C. Some Hispanics came to the United States as refugees. A refugee is a person who leaves one country to seek safety in another country. Many Hispanic Americans live in the Adams-Morgan neighborhood.

About 31,000 Washingtonians have Hispanic backgrounds. Most of Washington's Hispanics are from Central and South American countries. Many are from El Salvador. Washington, D.C., has a larger percentage of Salvadorans than any U.S. state.

About 11,000 Asian Americans live in Washington, D.C.

Asian Americans

Asian Americans are another fast-growing group in Washington, D.C. Many Asian Americans also live in the Adams-Morgan neighborhood.

About 11,000 Asian Americans live in Washington. Many Asian American families came from China, India, or Japan. Recently, Vietnamese and Cambodian refugees have come to Washington.

Chapter 4

The History of Washington, D.C.

Native Americans once lived in the area that is now Washington, D.C. They were mostly Piscataway people.

By 1680, many had left the area. By then, English colonists had built tobacco plantations there. A colonist is someone who lives in a newly settled area. The area that is now Washington was part of the Maryland colony.

The Revolutionary War

By 1732, England had 13 colonies along the Atlantic Coast. In the 1760s, England tightened its control of them. The colonists declared their

Washington, D.C., was named after George Washington.

In 1787, American leaders wrote the U.S. Constitution.

independence in 1776. This led to the
Revolutionary War (1776-1783).

The colonies won their independence from
England. They became the United States of
America. The new nation did not settle in a
permanent capital. The government moved
from city to city until 1800.

A Permanent Capital
In 1787, American leaders wrote the
Constitution of the United States. The

Constitution is a set of rules for government. One part called for a permanent capital.

The leaders decided the capital should not be part of any state. They feared the state containing the capital would have too much power. So they decided to create a separate district. This district would belong to all the states.

In 1791, President George Washington picked the site for the new capital. The people of Maryland and Virginia gave up land for the district. This land was near the Potomac River. This land became the District of Columbia. The district covered 100 square miles (259 square kilometers).

A Planned City

President Washington chose Pierre-Charles L'Enfant to plan the capital. L'Enfant was a French city planner. His plan showed wide streets and a long mall. He placed the Capitol at the center of the city.

Today, parts of Washington, D.C., look much like L'Enfant's plan. His plan did not allow for two events, however.

First, the population of the city grew quickly. People needed places to live. Some people built neighborhoods without checking L'Enfant's plan.

Second, the district gave part of the original land back to Virginia in 1846. The people and buildings on that land became part of Virginia. Today, the district covers just 68 square miles (176.8 square kilometers).

Early Years

In 1800, the federal government moved to Washington, D.C. But lawmakers did not meet in the Capitol. People were just beginning to build it.

In 1802, Congress allowed Washingtonians to elect a city council. By 1820, the federal government allowed Washingtonians to elect their own mayor.

However, Washingtonians could not vote for president. They could not elect representatives to Congress. Those rights belonged only to people who lived in the states.

Washingtonians rebuilt the U.S. Capitol after the War of 1812.

The War of 1812

In 1812, the United States and England went to war again. In 1814, English troops burned the unfinished Capitol and other buildings. The United States won the war in 1815.

Washingtonians began rebuilding their city. Many people moved to Washington to help rebuild the city. By 1850, almost 52,000 people lived in Washington.

The Civil War

By 1860, the issue of slavery divided the nation. Most people in northern states wanted slavery to be illegal. Most people in southern states wanted slavery to be legal.

In 1860 and 1861, 11 southern states broke away from the United States. These states formed a new country called the Confederate States of America. This led to the Civil War. The Union was made up of the states that were still a part of the United States.

Abraham Lincoln was president during the Civil War.

The Civil War ended April 9, 1865. The Union won. Six days later, John Wilkes Booth killed President Lincoln in Washington. Booth was a southerner upset about the outcome of the Civil War. In December 1865, the U.S. government freed all slaves in the country.

Changes in the City

Between 1870 and 1890, 100,000 people moved to Washington, D.C. Many were African Americans.

In 1871, the elected city council became a territorial government. The president appointed these leaders. This government oversaw building projects in the city. The projects included new streets and sidewalks. This government ran out of money, however.

In 1874, Congress ended Washington's territorial government. The president appointed three officials to run the city.

Congress oversaw major building projects in Washington. Builders started working on the Library of Congress and the Lincoln Memorial. They finished the Washington Monument.

Continued Growth

The federal government grew larger between 1917 and 1945. It led the nation through two world wars. Government leaders also set up the New Deal (1933-1939). This program created many jobs. It helped people during the hard times of the Great Depression (1929-1939).

Thousands of people came to Washington between 1917 and 1945. Many came to work for the government. Washington had a building boom. A boom is a rapid increase. Builders built housing, offices, and schools for the new Washingtonians.

The government completed the Supreme Court Building and the Lincoln and Thomas Jefferson Memorials. Jefferson was the third president of the United States.

The Government of Washington, D.C.

In 1963, Washingtonians gained the right to vote for the president. In 1970, they gained the right to elect a representative to Congress. This person could not vote on laws. Washingtonians gained the right to elect a mayor and city council in 1973.

Builders completed the Supreme Court Building in 1935.

In the early 1990s, some people wanted the District of Columbia to become the 51st state. They wanted to name the state New Columbia. Congress did not make New Columbia a state.

In the mid-1990s, Washington, D.C., had many problems. Streets needed repairs. There were few teachers and books for students. In 1997, Congress appointed a control board. Board members worked with the mayor and city council. They oversaw efforts to solve the city's problems.

Chapter 5

Business in Washington, D.C.

The federal government is the biggest business in Washington, D.C. About 160,000 people are federal workers. This is more than half of the city's workforce.

Other people work in lobbying, tourism, or manufacturing. Lobbying means trying to convince people in government to vote a certain way. Tourism is the city's biggest service business.

The incomes of workers in Washington are among the nation's highest. Income is the amount of money a person earns in a year. In 1995, the average income per person was about $32,000.

Tourism is Washington's biggest service business. Many tourists visit the White House each year.

Federal workers earned an average of $52,000 that year.

Some Washingtonians do not have jobs. In 1995, more than 40,000 people did not have jobs.

U.S. Government Workers

The president and members of Congress work for the U.S. government. So do the justices of the Supreme Court. Many people work for these officials. They include writers, secretaries, and lawyers. Many people work for other government departments as well.

Thousands of lobbyists work in Washington. They do not work for the U.S. government. They represent businesses and other groups. Lobbyists try to affect the nation's lawmakers. They want laws passed that help the groups they represent.

Tourism

Tourism is Washington's second-largest business. Each year, tourists spend more than $5 billion in Washington. Hotels, restaurants, and shops receive many tourist dollars.

Other people work with tourists. Guides give tourists information about Washington. Guards

Bus drivers take tourists around the city.

protect public buildings in Washington. Bus
drivers take tourists around the city.

Manufacturing

Printing and publishing are Washington's
leading manufacturing businesses. Several
well-known magazines are published there.
National Geographic is one of them. *U.S. News
and World Report* is another.

The Government Printing Office is in
Washington, D.C. It prints items such as books
and official records for the U.S. government.

Chapter 6

Seeing the Sights

Many historic events have happened in Washington, D.C. Many visitors want to see the places where these events happened. Visitors also go to museums and monuments. Museums have many historic objects. Monuments honor people who were important in the nation's history. Visitors also tour government buildings.

Museums and the National Zoo

The Smithsonian Institution is a group of museums. The museums contain displays of art, history, and science. Smithsonian museums have about 140 million objects. The objects are

Visitors tour monuments and government buildings.

from the United States and countries throughout the world.

There are many Smithsonian museums. The National Museum of African Art has carvings, masks, and clay pots. The National Air and Space Museum shows the history of flight. Dinosaur skeletons stand in the National Museum of Natural History.

The National Archives holds many important government records. Visitors can see the original Constitution of the United States there.

In 1993, the U.S. Holocaust Memorial Museum opened. The museum shows the history of Jewish people in Europe during World War II. The German government killed millions of Jewish people during World War II. The museum displays art, photographs, and personal objects of those who died. Personal objects include eye glasses, shoes, clothes, and suitcases.

Visitors to the Capital Children's Museum learn about music, television, and art. Visitors also learn about other countries.

SEEK TO ESTABLISH
OVERNMENT BASED ON
NTATION OF ALL HUMAN
ANDFUL OF INDIVIDUAL
L THIS A NEW ORDER.
V AND IT IS NOT ORDER.

The Franklin Delano Roosevelt Memorial features gardens with statues of Roosevelt.

More than 5,000 animals live in the National Zoological Park. Visitors to the zoo can see a giant panda, apes, elephants, and other animals.

Monuments

The John F. Kennedy Center for the Performing Arts holds ballets, concerts, and plays. The center is a monument that honors John F. Kennedy. He was the 35th president of the United States.

The Vietnam Veterans Memorial is at the west end of the National Mall. It honors people who died in the Vietnam War (1954-1975).

The Thomas Jefferson Memorial is located at the Tidal Basin. A bronze statue of Jefferson stands at the memorial's center.

The Franklin Delano Roosevelt Memorial is also at the Tidal Basin. It features gardens with statues of Roosevelt. He was the 32nd president of the United States. He started the New Deal. He led the nation during World War II.

Government and Historic Buildings

The Federal Bureau of Investigation (FBI) is a government agency. At FBI headquarters, visitors learn how the FBI solves crimes.

The White House is the president's home. The president's office and other offices are also there. Visitors can tour seven of the 132 rooms in the White House.

Embassy Row is a two-mile (3.2-kilometer) stretch of Massachusetts Avenue. Many foreign embassies line this street. Several embassies open for tours on the second Saturday in May.

The Bureau of Engraving and Printing prints about $22 million each day.

At the Bureau of Engraving and Printing, visitors can watch as the nation's paper money is made. The Bureau prints about $22 million each day.

Ford's Theatre is the place where John Wilkes Booth shot President Lincoln. The Petersen House is across the street from Ford's Theatre. There, visitors see the bed where Lincoln died.

Time Line

1600—Piscataway people are living in the Washington, D.C., area.

1632—The land that is now Washington, D.C., becomes part of the Maryland colony.

1775-1783—During the Revolutionary War, the 13 colonies fight for independence from England.

1787—The U.S. Constitution calls for a permanent national capital.

1791—President George Washington chooses the site of the nation's capital.

1800—The nation's government moves to Washington, D.C.

1802—Congress lets Washingtonians elect a city council.

1814—The English invade the capital and burn several buildings during the War of 1812.

1846—The Smithsonian Institution is founded.

1861—The Civil War begins.

1862—President Abraham Lincoln ends slavery in Washington, D.C.

1865—The Union wins the Civil War; John Wilkes Booth kills President Lincoln at Ford's Theatre; the U.S. government ends slavery in the nation.

1878—Congress ends the territorial government; the president appoints people to run the city.

1888—The Washington Monument opens to the public.

1914—The Lincoln Memorial is completed.

1935—The Supreme Court Building is completed.

1943—The Jefferson Memorial is completed.

1963—Washingtonians gain the right to vote for the president of the United States.

1967—The president appoints a mayor and city council for Washington, D.C.

1970—Washingtonians gain the right to elect a non-voting representative to Congress.

1973—Congress allows Washingtonians to elect a mayor and city council.

1990—Sharon Pratt Kelly becomes the first female mayor of Washington, D.C.

1992—The U.S. House of Representatives approves statehood for Washington, D.C. The Senate does not act on the issue.

1995—Nation of Islam leader Louis Farrakhan holds the Million Man March at the National Mall.

1997—The Franklin Delano Roosevelt Memorial opens.

Famous Washingtonians

Ann Beattie (1947-) Novelist and short story writer whose works include *Falling in Place* and *Picturing Will*.

Carl Bernstein (1944-) Reporter for *The Washington Post* who helped uncover the Watergate scandal (1974); co-wrote *All the President's Men* with Bob Woodward.

Billie Burke (1885-1970) Actress best known for her role as Glinda the Good Witch in *The Wizard of Oz*.

Connie Chung (1946-) Television reporter and news anchor who has worked for CBS and NBC.

Benjamin Oliver Davis (1877-1970) Army officer who became the first African American general in the U.S. Army (1940).

Benjamin Oliver Davis Jr. (1912-) Air Force officer who was the first African American general in the U.S. Air Force (1965).

John Foster Dulles (1888-1959) Statesman who helped found the United Nations (1944-1945); served as U.S. secretary of state (1953-1959).

Helen Hayes (1900-1993) Actress on Broadway, in movies, and on television.

J. Edgar Hoover (1895-1972) Government official who became the first director of the Federal Bureau of Investigation (1924-1972).

Sharon Pratt Kelly (1944-) First female mayor of Washington, D.C. (1991-1995).

Sugar Ray Leonard (1956-) Boxer who won a gold medal at the 1976 Olympic Games; won six world championship titles.

Chita Rivera (1933-) Actress, singer, and dancer who starred in the Broadway musicals *West Side Story* and *Bye, Bye Birdie*.

John Philip Sousa (1854-1932) Bandleader and composer; led the Marine Band (1880-1892).

Words to Know

boom (BOOM)—a rapid increase

capital (KAP-uh-tuhl)—a city that is an official center of government

capitol (KAP-uh-tuhl)—a building where lawmakers meet

colonist (KOL-uh-nist)—someone who lives in a newly settled area

embassy (EM-buh-see)—a building where representatives from another country work

lobbying (LOB-ee-ing)—trying to convince people in government to vote a certain way

mall (MAWL)—a long, grassy area

marsh (MARSH)—an area of low, wet land

piedmont (PEED-mont)—at the foot of a mountain

plantation (plan-TAY-shuhn)—a large farm

refugee (REF-yuh-jee)—a person who leaves one country for the safety of another

tidal basin (TIDE-uhl BAY-suhn)—a low area near a river that takes in flood water

To Learn More

Brill, Marlene Targ. *Building the Capital City*. Chicago: Children's Press, 1996.

Guzzetti, Paula. *The White House*. Parsippany, N.J.: Dillon Press, 1996.

Rubin, Beth. *Washington, D.C., with Kids*. A Frommer's Family Travel Guide. New York: Macmillan Travel, 1996.

Santella, Andrew. *The Capitol*. Chicago: Children's Press, 1995.

Internet Sites

Excite Travel: Washington, D.C.
http://city.net/countries/united_states/
district_of_columbia/washington/

TRAVEL.org — Washington D.C.
http://travel.org/dc.html

Welcome to the White House
http://www.whitehouse.gov

The Smithsonian Institution Home Page
http://www.si.edu/newstart.htm

Useful Addresses

The Capital Children's Museum
800 3rd St., NE
Washington, DC 20002

Library of Congress
101 Independence Ave., SE
Washington, DC 20540

Smithsonian Institution Information Center
1000 Jefferson Drive, SW
Washington, DC 20560

Many people visit the Vietnam Veterans Memorial each year.

Index